ADVICE TO MY CHILD

241 Things my parents should have told me, but didn't.

By Thomas C. McDaniel III
presented by Mb McDaniel Zellon

Library of Congress Control Number:		2023903601
ISBN:	Hardcover	978-1-6698-6871-2
	Softcover	978-1-6698-6872-9
	eBook	978-1-6698-6873-6

Print information available on the last page.

Rev. date: 06/23/2023

To order additional copies of this book, contact:
Xlibris
844-714-8691
www.Xlibris.com
Orders@Xlibris.com
851483

Preface

In 2014, my brother, Thomas C. McDaniel III, gave me a copy of a manuscript he had written. He wanted me to read it and share my thoughts. Tom was an excellent writer but I had no idea he had been working on a manuscript. When I read through it, I liked it. Not thinking much at the time, I put it aside and didn't think about it again...until four years later.

I am Marybeth McDaniel Zellon, Tom's sister. We are Irish twins actually, born 18 months apart. As children, Tom and I were very close. As teenagers we shared the same friends and did most things together. As adults, we remained close.

Fast forward to October of 2018. Tom knocked on my front door one morning around 10am. I hadn't seen him or spoken to him in a while as we were in a silly sibling fight. That morning he was in tremendous pain and didn't feel well. Despite having not spoken to each other in a few months, he turned to me for help when he needed it most.

I got Tom to the hospital and it was discovered that he had advanced Colon cancer that had already spread. He was gone 2 months later. There is a valuable lesson here for all of us: Don't ignore symptoms and get a Colonoscopy! It could save your life!

The day that I took Tom to the hospital I am sure he didn't think that would be the last time he would walk out of the home he had lived in for 24 years. Yet, it was.

The responsibility of cleaning out my brother's house fell to me, as our 2 other sisters lived out of state. It took me a year to clean out the home, make small repairs and prepare it for renting. During this clean-out I found a hard copy of the manuscript, thinking this information is for his child. Tom is survived by his only son, who was 9-years-old when his dad passed. Ironically, the same age Tom was when our mother died unexpectedly in 1967. Tom was 9 and I was 7½ when she passed. Life can be strange.

Having discovered the manuscript tucked away in a drawer I came to think that my dear brother sensed his fate and wanted to impart wisdom and direction on his son before he passed. Tom must have known he was not long for this world.

Therefore, today I am honored (and feel a sense of responsibility) to ensure his son gets this advice. Since most of the content you are about to read is very real, mature, and at times painfully direct, I had to wait a few years to give this to his son. Much of the advice was too advanced for a 9-year-old. But perhaps now, his teenage son can read it for himself and understand his father a little better.

My hopes are that this manuscript serves as a discussion point for his son to ask and learn. I should state that I don't personally agree with every bit of advice Tom wrote. But they are his words, and his son should know them. Some advice is serious, some is laugh out loud funny. I hope that this manuscript, presented as a book, will serve other parents to open awkward discussions about the facts of life with their preteen and teenage children.

Ninety-nine percent of this book was written by my brother. I am merely a vessel to present, slightly edit, organize and funnel these bits of advice to the world.

I wish you health, happiness and understanding!

In your service,

Mb McDaniel Zellon – June 2023

1. Everyone feels fear. The trick is what you do with it.

Some have more, some have less, but everyone has fear. There are two things you can do with fear: you can let it paralyze you into inaction, or you can use it to motivate you into redoubling your efforts. Make it a positive that works for you rather than a negative that works against you.

2. You catch a lot more flies with honey, than you do with vinegar.

An old adage, but completely true. You don't ever need to be a jerk in life, although many people think you do. However, if you do decide to be a jerk, do it carefully and be quick to soften up and stop being a jerk.

3. Keep your options open.

Don't do things that close off doors. Keep your choices open for as long as you can. However, don't be afraid to commit. You will know the right time and if you are unsure, it isn't the right time yet.

4. There is no proof of the existence of God except possibly the existence of everything else.

Faith is a belief in the absence of proof. Nothing really proves God – in fact there are a whole lot of things that prove that He doesn't exist. But, all of creation taken in aggregate, how can you deny God exists ?

5. In negotiations, the trick is to get as much as much as you can without going too far and having the deal fall apart.

Deals most often fall apart because people get too greedy and go too far. It is a common rookie mistake to think you can get everything you want and give up nothing in return. Start way out in left field. Do not start close to the middle. Give yourself plenty of room to seemingly give up things to get in the middle.

6. If you don't have it by midnight, you are probably not going to get it.

A high school friend's father told him that.
Experience has taught me that it is true.

7. Don't brag even if you can do it.

No one likes to hear bragging – particularly from someone that can do it. As a rule of thumb, keep your mouth shut about your abilities. 88326461

8. Military historians say that a country should go to war only as an absolute last resort. Once started, a war is extremely difficult to stop. The same goes for fights, feuds, arguments, etc.

Once they get going, they have a life of their own that is difficult to bring to an end.

Thomas C. McDaniel III

9. Honesty is generally the best policy — except when it comes to dealing with the opposite sex.

Try answering questions - "what are you thinking?" "If I died, would you remarry?" "Do these pants make my butt look big?" -Now, do you think the honest answer is the best answer?

10. Don't be a jerk to a cop even if the cop is a jerk to you — which can be the case.

Bad things can happen and when they do, they are never in your favor. Remember: the cop has the badge, handcuffs, pepper spray, gun, and usually an attitude. Cops see things in black and white – you are either a criminal or you are a potential criminal. Act accordingly and know that you are not going to talk your way out of things. Keep your hands where the cop can see them and keep your mouth shut.

11. Make a list of things you have to do that day. Cross each off as you finish it.

When the list is finished, go have fun.

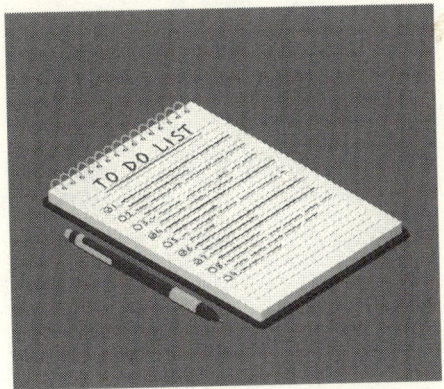

12. Drugs and alcohol are effective in the short term, but they are not worth it in the medium or long run. Keep your consumption to a minimum, or better yet, do them as little as you can or not at all. You will feel better, think better, and function better.

13. Exercise.

Exercise is great for the body, but it is just as good for your mind. It will surprise you how good it makes you feel afterwards each time you do it.

14. Do not go to extremes.

Try to balance mainstream without being boring.

15. Chances are you will not get what you want in life unless you actually speak up and tell people exactly what you want.

It is not generally a good thing to quote Madonna because no one has ever accused her of being an intellectual heavyweight, but Madonna happens to be right in this one particular instance. If you want something a certain way, you have to speak up and say out loud what you want. It isn't likely that things will work out exactly like you want by coincidence.

Thomas C. McDaniel III

16. Don't get married young.

Youthful marriages rarely work out. When you are young you have way too much to go through in life yet and you are going to make too many life changes to expect another person to understand everything and go in lock-step along with you. You are not going to be the same person at 20 that you will be at 30. Do yourself a favor and just skip marriage until you are at least 30.

17. Don't drink and drive – period. It isn't worth it if you get caught.

Every state allows you to drink and drive to a limit. Generally, it is legal to have a beer or two and drive a car. But, drinking even a little impairs you and you are quite capable of having an accident that injures some for life or even kills them. If you are lucky, you may get just a DUI. But, depending on the state you live in, that will cost you thousands of dollars and mean jail time, etc

18. Learn to dance and do it whenever you can.

It is good exercise and it is fun. Moreover, it is great way to meet and interact with members of the opposite sex.

19. Having a kid is probably the greatest thing that will ever happen to you.

20. Don't have kids just because you think that is part of having the full life experience.

21. Take care of your teeth and feet. Floss once a day. Spend the money to go to the dentist regularly and buy good shoes.

22. It is OK to not go to college

23. It is OK to not like cats, dogs, or kids. It is not a character flaw.

24. Joining the military can be a great idea. You serve your country and you can earn money to go to college. 20 years in the military can make sense too. You serve your country, travel, learn skills, and retire with a great pension and healthcare and you are still young enough to begin a whole new career. Moreover, a 20 year military career on

Thomas C. McDaniel III

your resume in priceless if you want to go into politics or a lot of things.

25. Don't buy anything but regular gas. Anything else is a waste of money because the car you drive probably doesn't need the higher octane.

26. Generally buy a used car and let the first owner take the depreciation.

27. Live like you are going to make it to 100 years old.

28. Put $1000 cash away for emergencies and do not touch it except in the direst need.

29. Keep in contact with old friends.

30. Give money or gift cards as gifts.

31. Do not forget your Significant Others birthday, Valentine's Day, or your anniversary.

32. If you decide to cheat on your Significant Other, plan now what you are going to say to them when you get caught – because almost certainly, you will get caught.

33. Don't do anything you know you will be embarrassed about later.

34. Don't worry what strangers think. You will never see them again.

35. If a woman tells you she has had sex with X amount of people, multiply that number by three. If a man tells you he has had sex with X amount of people, divide that number by three.

36. When dating, always go for sane and plain, over cute and crazy.

37. Live your life so that a lot of people will come to your funeral.

38. Carry a tire gauge in your glove box of your car.

39. Never wake a sleeping baby.

40. Don't use tobacco. It is smelly, stains your teeth, is bad for your health, and says, "I'm a dumb-ass."

41. Don't gamble more than you can afford to lose – which for most of us is $0.

42. Don't take stupid unnecessary physical risks.

43. Motorcycles are fun and cheap to drive, but if you have even a medium wreck, you are either dead or in the hospital for 6 months.

44. Learn to either play a musical instrument or speak a foreign language.

45. Travel as much as you can when you are young before you get married and have kids.

46. Have sex with a lot of different people as long as you are not in a committed relationship – but always use protection.

47. Beware of credit cards. Getting into debts is one hell of a lot easier than getting out of debt.

48. Find a mentor who will take you under their wing.

49. Don't give your kids stripper names like Sierra, Mercedes, or Tiffany, or give them last names as first names like Carter, Holden, or Jackson. Never give a girl a masculine name like Addison or Madison. When naming a kid, think first what a 3rd grade bully will do to the proposed name on the playground.

50. You are probably smarter and better looking than you think you are. You are probably a lot more attractive than you think you are.

51. Take a naked picture of yourself in the mirror when you are around nineteen. You will be glad you did when you look at it as the years pass.

52. While Patriotism is the last refuge of a scoundrel, don't be afraid to be patriotic and wave the flag. Just don't use your patriotism to justify jingoism.

53. When negotiating a price for an item, start high and don't come down fast. Don't be afraid to let them come to you rather than you going to them. Moreover, don't be afraid to walk away. More times than not, they will cave and call you back.

54. Go with your gut feelings about things. It is almost always right.

55. Be willing to compromise to make a deal everyone can live with. Moreover, if everyone is unhappy, that is probably the best deal.

56. A wise man learns from the mistakes of others, a fool has to learn it for himself.

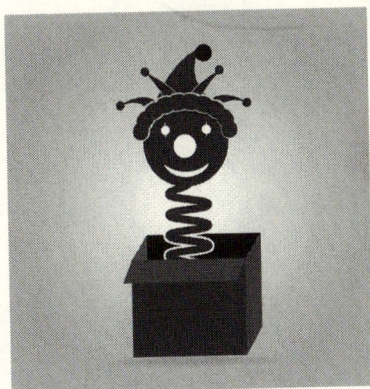

57. Be inclined to grant others mercy because you are going to need someone to give it to you someday.

58. We humans are fragile and we break.

59. Sometimes things get too broken to be fixed.

60. Age is just a number. However, keep in mind that you only get so many of those numbers.

61. Dating is a numbers game. Don't put all your dating eggs in one basket.

62. There is no such thing as a soul mate.

63. Being straight and clear-headed give you an edge over someone that is drunk or stoned.

Thomas C. McDaniel III

64. If you are winning, keep your mouth shut. You can't make it better. You can only make it worse.

65. Remember that most other people are probably less secure and confident than you are.

66. Losing weight is easy. All you have to do is eat less and exercise more.

67. It is not hard NOT to get pregnant.

68. The Sunday rules are

1) you can sleep as late as you want
2) you can wear sweatpants and a T-shirt with holes in it all day
3) nobody is allowed to make plans and
4) you can go back to bed without any explanation.

69. Family is not really about shared genetics. It is about love and a life-time commitment to each other.

70. If something is good enough, keep it. The bigger, better deal doesn't usually exist.

71. Never ask your significant other how many people they have had sex with.

72. Guitars will get you through tough times (of no money) better than getting you though tough times with no guitars.

73. Do not get in the passing lane and drive the speed limit.

74. It is OK to eat and enjoy a thick, medium-rare steak now and then.

75. Be on time. Being late shows contempt for other people's time.

76. It is OK to never get married or have kids. Don't think you have to do either to have a full life. Not everyone should get married and even fewer should have kids.

77. If you are FORCED to steal, make it worth the risk and effort. Steal $25 million, not $50.

78. Don't wear too much makeup or perfume and don't date someone who does.

I recall once being in a car with a woman on a cold, rainy night and having to roll down the window to get some fresh air. Some people apparently cannot tell when enough is enough.

79. Sign using blue ink. That way you can easily tell it's not a copy.

80. Two cats/dogs are actually easier to have than one as they will play with and entertain each other. Same with kids.

81. Talk slowly and enunciate each word as you say it. Don't talk with your hands unless you are using sign language.

82. There is nothing wrong with being gay.

83. Don't gossip.

84. Tip liberally.

85. If someone asks you for money on the street, if you have it, give it to them.

86. It is OK to co-sleep with your child. Mammals like chipmunks and dogs all sleep in a big pile. What mammal makes their baby sleep by itself in another room?

87. Keep your car registration and proof of insurance in an envelope in your glove box for quick and easy access when a cop demands them.

88. Keep your tax records in 12 manila folders – one for each month. Make a new one each month and fill it up as need be with receipts, paid invoices, and other tax documents that you need to keep. Then in April, pull out all 12 and do your taxes yourself.

89. Bad friends are not worth keeping. You can tell a bad friend by how painful they are to have as friends. A good friend is one that doesn't hurt. A bad friend is one that hurts.

90. Never let the weather stop you from doing something.

91. It actually does feel better to give, than receive.

92. The world can be divided into two: people who like pie and people who like cake.

93. It is not humanly possible to not like chocolate. If someone says they don't, don't believe them.

94. Look people right in the eyes when you talk to them.

95. Always be the first to end a telephone conversation.

96. Astrology is bogus. A lot of things people believe are bogus. There are no ghosts, vampires, big foots, chulpacabras, or zombies. Never suspend a healthy skepticism.

97. Cops are almost always jerks. Do not trust one – even off duty. However, firemen and paramedics are almost always great people.

98. Just because you don't know the answer, doesn't mean there isn't one.

99. If we are alone in the universe, then the Creator wasted one hell of a lot of space.

100. It is much better to be filthy rich and unhappy, than dirt poor and unhappy.

101. The goal of GM is not to make cars, it is to make money. They just happen to make cars to do it.

102. We all have these little castles of life. Your job is to protect and grow your life castle.

If someone breaks into your life castle and steals your stuff, you can look at it two ways:

1) it's the thief's fault for taking your stuff, or
2) you know thieves exist so it is completely your fault for letting a thief get into your life castle and take your stuff.

103. If the words "if" appears in an apology, it isn't really an apology.

104. Do not mistake sexual attraction for love.

105. When you begin a new and serious relationship, it is best to put off sex as long as possible. Do not rush. You will know when the time is right. It is better for it to have never been right than to rush it and regret it.

106. There are five ways to get money: steal it, win it, inherit it, marry it, or make it. All are about the same in value because money is money.

107. The world is not going to end tomorrow. Steer clear of anyone who thinks it is.

108. The world is not 6,000 years old and Adam and Eve did not ride around on dinosaurs. Steer clear of anyone who thinks it is and that they did.

109. Divorce and bankruptcy are the best laws on the books because they allow you to shake off the past and start over again new.

110. Give people a second chance, but not a third or fourth. America is all about second chances. All of our ancestors came to America because they weren't doing very well where they were and they wanted or needed a second chance.

111. Don't get into online relationships. You need to stare into someone's eyes, smell their breath, and hear them breathing.

112. If two people do something together and one is a man and the other is a woman, it's a date even if you want to call it something else.

Thomas C. McDaniel III

113. Gun ownership is about protection. Gun obsession is about power. The line between the two is usually determined by how many guns you possess.

114. Guns are unique and should be treated as such. Guns are extremely and exceptionally lethal.

115. Gasoline is unique and should be treated as such. Right now, everything runs on it in some way or another.

116. Suntans are out, but tan lines are sexy.

117. Women think men like skinny women. Men don't. They like healthy, normal looking women.

118. Wear a tie and jacket or a dress when possible.

The opposite sex thinks they look good.

119. Always eat something before you drink. If you drink on an empty stomach it will make you get sloppy drunk and no one likes a sloppy drunk.

120. Learn basis survival skills like grocery shopping, cooking, and doing
laundry, etc.

121. Long distance relationships do not work out. Exceptions are so rare they can be safely ignored.

122. When people sing, their accents disappear. However, American country music is they only music where the accent not only doesn't disappear, it is exaggerated.

123. Don't blow people off without an explanation.

124. There is a cosmic balance sheet with your name on it. If you do good things, good things will generally come back to you. If you do bad things, bad things will generally come back to bite you. However, it is not absolute. Some great people have horrible things happen to them and some horrible people do extremely well in life. Hitler got what he deserved. However, Stalin, who was every bit as horrible a person as Hitler, enjoyed an opulent lifestyle and wielded absolute power until the second he died.

125. History is full of examples of people who voluntarily renounce fame and/or power. However, there are absolutely no meaningful historical examples of anyone who fully renounced great wealth.

126. Weddings are exceptionally great places to hook up. People are looking good and feeling good and romance is in the air.

127. The best place to pick up women is in an arts and crafts store. Look helpless and ask a random attractive woman to help you find a gift for your sister who sews and knits a lot.

128. Having sex with someone generally complicates things a lot.

129. Don't have sex for the first time in your life until you are emotionally mature enough to handle it. For most of us, that is probably around age 18.

130. You don't have to prove anything to anybody.

131. Marriage is like comparing a lion in a zoo to a lion on the plains of Africa. In the zoo, the lion is fed three square meals a day, he gets free healthcare, female companionship abounds, and he gets lots of zoo keeper attention. It is an easy life, but at the end of the day, the lion is still in a cage. On the other hand, on the plains of Africa, the lion

has to hunt for food and usually goes hungry, there is no healthcare at all, poachers, hyenas, and other lions are trying to kill him, and females are hard to come by. It is a tough life, but at the end of the day, the lion is free.

132. A trophy wife is half your age plus seven years and it proves the old adage that there is no fool like an old fool. All you can hope for is that the old fool gets a lot of bang for his buck.

133. Never admit anything – particularly in politics and relationships.

134. Don't snitch, narc, tattle, rat-out or otherwise tell on someone.

135. The definition of hero is someone who runs towards danger rather than away from it.

136. If you feel sick, rest and food are usually all you need to feel significantly better. The body seeks to heal itself... if you treat it right.

137. There is only one race: the human race.

138. Go to church on occasion. It clears your head and it is good to consider a higher power now and then.

139. Tell the people you love that you love them.

140. Have fun. Other people are attracted to people who are having fun and want to be a part of that fun.

141. Each day, try to do at least one thing to improve yourself, your relationships, and your business.

142. Do not buy extended warranties. Nine times out of ten, they are complete rip-offs.

143. Do not let a doctor prescribe you medication. Once you are on the medication treadmill, you are eventually going to find yourself taking ten medications or more. Tell your doctor that it is against your religion to take drugs or medication and that his job is to treat your particular malady without prescribing drugs.

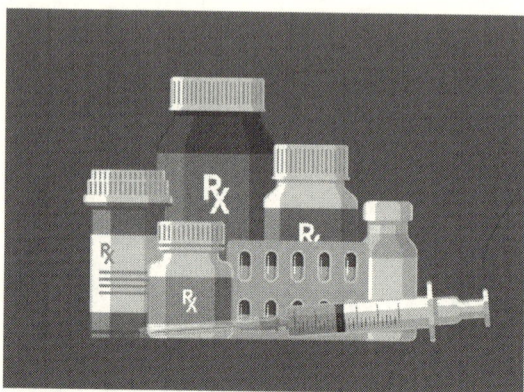

144. Hospitals are hellholes. As a patient, you want to stay in a hospital as briefly as humanly possible - and avoid them altogether if possible. The job of a hospital is to patch you up and get you home as quickly as possible to recover in peace at home. The only time a hospital is OK is when are actually escaping an even bigger hellhole like war. Then, it is perfectly OK to stay in the hospital as long as you can contrive to and rest up, eat up, and flirt with nurses.

145. A sexless marriage is like a sandwich made of two pieces of bread with nothing in between them.

146. I have now been on both sides of testosterone: having too much of it and not having enough. Women have no clue

Thomas C. McDaniel III

how incredibly powerful testosterone is and they have no right to judge until they themselves experience it.

147. It is true that the squeaky wheel gets the grease, so do not be afraid to squeak. However, when you do squeak, make sure that you do it with honey in your voice and manner.

148. Once is an aberration. Twice is a syndrome.

149. Always have a woman or a gay man cut your hair. Never get your hair cut by a straight man – unless you are actually going for the military haircut look.

150. Steer clear of anyone that a friend or a family member has already dated. However, if you are hell bent on still dating that person, ask and receive clear permission first.

151. Psychics are complete phonies. If there was anything to predict it was 9/11. No one did. What more proof do you need?

152. A marriage license is not just a piece of paper. If anyone thinks it is, they need to immediately consult with a family law attorney to be completely disabused of the ridiculous notion.

153. It is much better to dump than to be dumped. Break up with them before they break up with you. Get them before they get you.

154. Ideally, date someone who likes you just as much as you like them. If that is not possible, try to date someone who likes you a little more than you like them.

155. Men generally only want two things in life: to get paid and to get laid. If a male gets those two things accomplished on a semi-regular basis, he's a totally happy camper. Men are just not that complex and don't have sophisticated needs. Of course, the ultimate man fantasy is to get paid to get laid. But, that opportunity is extremely rare. Has its own substantial downside (you are forever labeled a porn star), and most of us don't live anywhere near Los Angeles.

156. Men generally only think about three things: I'm hungry, I'm horny, and I'm sleepy.

Usually in that order too. Men are not nearly as deep as women give them credit for. When women think men are lost deep in though pondering particle physics or the meaning of a Shakespearean sonnet, the truth is that men are usually just thinking that they have to pee or wondering if they remember where they parked.

157. It is entirely possible to be too rich and too skinny.

The super-starved Auschwitz look is honestly just not very attractive. Moreover, we have all unfortunately run into people who have far too much money for their own good (and everyone else's) and have a lot more dollars in the bank, than sense between their ears.

158. Learn to think about nothing.

Being able to clear your mind of all thoughts is extremely useful, particularly when you are trying to fall asleep. Learn to clear your mind of everything. Some people call it counting sheep. The last thing you need is a mind full of racing thoughts that circle around endlessly. Take charge of your thoughts. You are in control of your own mind.

159. If you are not sure if you are in love, you aren't

You'll know it when you are. The feeling is pretty obvious. You can't mistake it for something else.

160. The fastest was to get over a broken heart is to find someone new.

If you get your heart broken, do not lie around and wallow in you misery. That is not going to do you any good and it only makes pain worse. Get back on the horse, as they say, and get busy.

161. Be understanding when you see weakness in other people.

The hope that they, in turn, will be understanding and gentle when they see weakness in you – and don't think that you don't have any weaknesses because you very likely have more than you think.

Thomas C. McDaniel III

162. It is best to believe that God exists.

If God does exist and you believe in him, then you are good. If God doesn't exist, then it really doesn't matter if you believe in him or not. However, if God does exist, and you don't believe in him, then you are probably really screwed.

163. An engagement ring is a condition gift and should be returned to the giver if the condition (marriage) doesn't happen.

Most women will see an engagement ring as an absolutely unconditional gift, i.e. they get to keep it no matter what happens – even if they themselves break off the engagement.

However, times have changed since the dark ages. Gifts in anticipation of marriage should be mutual and of the same approximate value: you give her an engagement ring, she gives you a big screen TV, and everyone goes home happy.

164. Things are usually not as bad as you think they are.

Imagination almost always gets the best of us. We nearly always trick up our imagination the thought that things are much worse than they really are – and that freaks us out. Don't be afraid of finding out the true state of things – because nearly always, you will be relieved. Of course, there is that very rare occasion when things are actually worse than you thought. But, don't let that scare you off. The odds are 99 to 1 that things are far better than you think.

165. Aspire to live in a world where everyone has the right to be happy.

If there is slavery, for example, the people who are slaves are not going to be happy. That means no matter what race, religion, sexual orientation or anything else, your society should allow you by its laws and morals to find your own happiness.

166. Try not to be an asshole.

Do I really need to explain that one?

167. There is actually such a thing as karma.

Karma really exists. If you do bad things, bad energy is going to back to you triple fold. If you do good things, you are going to get good things back triple fold.

168. Life is way to short to be unhappy.

169. Don't be a victim.

Thomas C. McDaniel III

170. Don't let a birthday bum you out. Carefully consider the alternative.

171. Don't take your own advice until you are positive that you are old enough and wise enough to give it to yourself.

Wait until you are at least 30 before you start taking your own advice. Always talk things over with other people and learn the general consensus before you make a decision.

172. You have to become the person that you want to be.

You don't just luck into becoming the person that you want to be. You have to work for it. First, identify what kind of person you want to be in life and then work towards becoming that person. It can be very hard and take a very long time, but ultimately it is always worth it.

173. Your highest priority in life is to find peace and happiness; you cannot put a price on peace and happiness.

174. Exercise. Not only is it good for you physically, but more importantly, you will be surprised how good it is for you mentally. Exercise creates a mental calmness and clarity that nothing else comes close to.

175. Showers are better than baths.

With showers, your stink goes down the drain. With baths, you stew in your own juices.

176. Manscape... Please!

No one likes to see hair sticking out of someone else's nostrils. Don't go overboard and turn into a metro sexual, but do get a hair trimmer and a nose clipper and use them both on a semi- regular basis. Besides, your wife/GF will like it.

177. Do not swear in public. It makes you look uneducated.

178. While you want to live a long life, you don't want to outlive your life.

179. Be patient.

180. It is better to be overdressed than under dressed. When in doubt, go overdressed.

181. Dress for the weather.

182. Eat out on Friday nights.

183. Don't be "that guy".

184. Never take legal advice from a cop.

Very few cops have gone to law school. You are probably never going to run into one that has. Cops may think they know the law, but they rarely actually do – even with stuff they deal with all the time like speeding and protective orders. The rule of thumb is that a cop is more likely to be wrong than right.

185. Beware men who wear yellow ties.

I'm not sure exactly why, but good rarely comes from a man wearing a yellow tie.

186. Money is always an object.

Unless they are Bill Gates (and probably even then too), when someone says, "money is no object", do not believe them because it always is. Always.

187. The best things in life usually don't cost much and work great.

188. Always try to focus on what you did right rather than what you did wrong.

Do not drive yourself crazy repeating things over and over in your head. Rather, focus on what you did right. Take a moment to congratulate yourself, and then move on. Learn from your mistakes, but do not obsess over them.

189. If someone says, "I'd really like to help you" that means that they are exactly the least likely source of any help.

190. There is no formula for a good marriage.

You can live with someone for ten years, get married, and be miserable - and you can know someone for ten days, get married, and be happy for the rest of your life. It is completely unpredictable.

91. A parent's love for a child is most like an owner's love for his/her pet.

The love that parent feels for a child is not like the love they feel for their parents, siblings, spouses, or friends. All those relationships are conditional in some way.

However, the love a parent feels for their child is unconditional, irrational, unwavering, and total.

That is most similar to what a pet owner feels for their pet. That love is also, unconditional, irrational, unwavering, and total.

192. Don't be afraid to admit when you are wrong.

Contrary to what John Wayne said in a movie, an apology is a sign of strength, not weakness.

193. Don't put bumper stickers on your car. However, if you are hell bent on doing so, at least don't put them on the paint.

194. Take care and protect your body.

195. Money is not vulgar.

As the old story says, money does not smell. Respect those that hustle to make money. Making money in a legal and ethical way is a hard thing to do and should be honored.

196. You have to feel your feelings.

You can ignore the feelings and you drown them in drink or mask them with drugs or just ignore them. But, sooner or later, you are going to have to face up to them like a man and deal with them. If you try to hide from them forever, you are just going to make it much worse. The only way to get to the other side and into the clear is to feel them.

197. Children are least able to deal with change.

I have heard some foolish people say that children are extremely resilient and are able to deal easily with change. That is hogwash and usually wishful thinking... Experience has told me the exact opposite is true.

198. Children are not small adults.

Children do not experience things like adults. Children are much less sophisticated and have only limited (if any) prior experience. Things are much bigger or much smaller for them than they are for adults.

199. Try to find someone who is in the same position in life as you are rather than just someone who is your own age.

200. You actually can change the past

We've all heard people say, "you can't change the past." That is not exactly true. While you cannot change the facts about the past, you can change how those facts are perceived today and in the future. If you learn something from a past event and allow it to change you and your behavior, then you actually change the past. If you don't learn anything and you won't or can't change, then you are letting the past victimize you and you are right – you can't change the past because you won't let it change you.

201. Respect other people's time.

If another person says they have only so much time to talk, or to please make it brief, quick, or short, then do so. Do not ignore them and drone on and on. Be sensitive to the other person trying to wind down the conversation. That other person is busy. Acknowledge that and act accordingly.

202. Thick letters usually are good news while thin letter are usually bad news.

Of course, it mostly depends on who the letter is from. No letter from the IRS or the State Bar should ever be put on the "read later" pile.

203. There are no answers at the bottom of a bottle of booze.

I used to call it "drinking and thinking." I thought that I could do some good thinking while I was drinking. The truth is that drinking would make me avoid thinking, not think better.

Drinking almost always causes more problems that is solves.

204. Just because you can do something doesn't necessarily mean you should. Important parts of maturing are learning restraint and discretion. Sometimes it is best to stay silent about something and just stay out of it. Ask yourself is this really, really my business?

Does it directly concern me or someone in my immediate family? If not, keep away and shut your mouth.

205. Women usually have a far different definition of cheating than men.

Men usually define cheating very narrowly. Unless there is penile/vaginal contact, it isn't cheating. On the other hand, women usually define cheating as including both physical and emotional cheating. To many women, going to a strip club, looking at internet porn, or even casually talking to a woman online is cheating.

206. Determine what you really love to do and then figure out some way to get paid to do it.

207. Get the money up front.

208. Do not be afraid to cut your losses.

NEVER throw good money after bad.

If there is any doubt in your mind, cut your losses and get the hell out. It is far better to get out too fast than stay too long.

209. If you lend money to someone, do not expect to get it back

Consider it a gift. Then, if you are paid back, you will be pleasantly surprised and have a good day.

210. The dividing line between childhood and adulthood is your attitude about sleep.

When you are a child, you never want to go to sleep. When you are an adult, you look forward to getting sleep.

211. A very key element to success in anything (business, school, etc) is to be completely on top of things.

Make your affairs be as tight as a drum. Do not let anything slide. Get on top of things and stay there. Get ahead if you can.

212. Beware deceptive appearances.

Thomas C. McDaniel III

People rarely appear bad and then turn out to be good once you get to know them. It happens, but not that often and the consequences are not disastrous of you get it wrong. However, beware of people who appear good but aren't. Steer clear of people who flatter, brown-nose, suck-up or place their religiousness right up front. If you get it wrong, those people can do you serious damage. Of course, that is why they do it. They hope that you drop your guard and they can sail in and exploit your defenselessness.

213. Get an education or a trade so that you can support yourself.

Do not under any circumstances allow yourself to become dependent on someone else.

214. Don't rubber-neck.

Use the gas pedal, get a move on and don't slow down traffic. People behind you have places to go and need to get there.

215. Don't laugh at your own jokes.

First, they may not be as funny as you think they are and secondly, let others decided whether they are funny or not.

216. Make real cranberry sauce for Thanksgiving dinner.

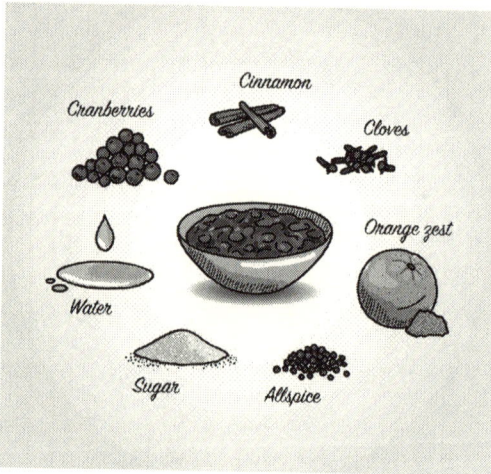

Real cranberry sauce is super easy to make and you get credit like you did something really hard-which you didn't.

217. A big part of growing up is learning that adults (particularly your parents) were right a lot more of the time than you had previously given them credit.

218. Assume that with a married couple, or even a boyfriend-girlfriend, what one person knows, the other person knows, too.

219. If you really want to keep a secret a secret, then don't tell anyone – not even your spouse.

220. Get all of the party out of your system before you settle down and have kids.

221. You do stupid things when you are in love.

Does that make those stupid thing OK, because you are in love? No, they are still stupid and you should know better. Realize that when you are in love, you are going to act stupid. So, bear that in mind and keep the stupid to a minimum.

223. Couples need intimacy to stay strong as a couple.

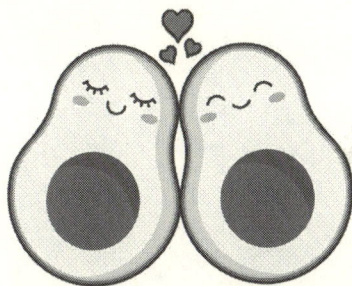

AVO-CUDDLE

224. Learn history so that you can recognize the patterns of life.

As said long ago, history repeats itself over and over and over, The same patterns in human behavior repeat over and over again because, while relatively complex life forms, humans just aren't very unique. We tend to do the same things repeatedly.

225. People do not change.

It takes a profound, near-death-like experience for someone to really change. Absent that, change is superficial at best.

226. At the end of your life, what you are probably likely to regret most is not what you did, but rather, what you didn't do.

227. The only thing that will matter ten thousand generations from now is if your own genes are still sloshing around somewhere in the gene pool.

228. If you don't know what to do, don't do anything.

229. The world is full of crazy, screwed up people.

Messed up people are probably much more common that you think. When trying to analyze a person's actions, as part of your analysis always consider the possibility that they are acting irrationally and that you are just not capable of understanding them.

230. Learn to relax and calm yourself.

Take a few deep breaths; consciously slow down your heart rate, un-tense your muscles. Learn progressive relaxation. As Shakespeare wrote in Hamlet, "there is noting either good or bad but thinking makes it so." Do not become a prisoner of your own thinking.

231. Rebates are intentionally hard to get.

The people in charge of designing a rebate offer don't want you to get the rebate. They make it intentionally onerous for you to get the rebate. Don't let them win. Do what you have to do to get the rebate.

232. If you think something is wrong, it almost always is. However, if you think something is right, it may or may not be that way.

233. The only person that you owe anything to is your child.

You owe nothing to your parents, siblings, other family members, friends, acquaintances and certainly not strangers. However, you owe your child everything – including your life. They didn't ask to be born and you brought them here for your own reasons.

234. Don't sell assets. The goal is to accumulate things, not divest them.

235. Some people don't deserve to be let off the hook.

Some say in it good to forgive and forget. Usually, that is the case. However, in very rare cases, there are injuries so deep and so profound that they should rightly never be forgiven. Should the Jews forgive and forget Adolf Hitler? No, they should not.

236. Suicide is never the answer.

237. Try to read the newspaper and stay up on the news at a minimum once a week so that you know at least a little of what is going on in the world.

238. It is far better to believe in God than not.

239. Love never comes when you are looking for it.

It will sneak up on you when you least expect it and it will come from a direction that you do not anticipate.

240. Everything has a beginning, middle, and end.

241. Know history. It can and does repeat itself.

Thomas C. McDaniel III

Made in the USA
Middletown, DE
14 June 2024